P9-DGZ-265

TURN EVERYTHING TO LOVE

A RULE OF LIFE FOR LAY MEMBERS OF THE VINCENTIAN FAMILY

Robert P. Maloney, C.M.

Title: **Turn Everything to Love**
Originally published in English and Spanish by:
Editorial La Milagrosa
Garcia de Paredes, 45
28010 Madrid

ISBN: 84-85076-65-6
Printed in the U.S.A.
February 2008

CONTENTS

---

[1] Throughout this Rule, SV refers to the fourteen-volume French edition of Saint Vincent's works, Correspondence, entretiens, documents, edited by Pierre Coste (Paris: Gabalda, 1920-25). CR refers to the Common Rules that St. Vincent wrote for the Congregation of the Mission and published, after many years of experimentation, in 1658.

LOVE IS INVENTIVE,
EVEN TO INFINITY.

SV XI, 146

FOREWORD

Do you wish to live more deeply as a lay member of the Vincentian Family? Then, I offer you this little book. It is not a study to shed light on unknown themes, nor a novel to stir your emotions. Rather, it is a Rule for daily life, based on the scriptures. I hope that it will help you to love God with all your heart, all your soul, all your mind, and all your strength, and to love your neighbor as yourself. As Jesus states clearly, that is what Christian life is all about.

Rules have a hallowed place in the Catholic tradition, particularly in the history of religious communities. The Rule of St. Benedict has enriched the lives of countless men and women for fifteen centuries. Other Rules, like those of St. Francis, St. Ignatius of Loyola and St. Vincent de Paul, have guided the daily actions of thousands of priests, brothers, and sisters during the last millennium. Modern rules like the Rule of Taizé and the beautifully written Rule for a New Brother have captured the imaginations of many.

But, different from these, the Rule that I propose to you focuses on lay men and women who belong to our Vincentian Family and whose love of God and love of neighbor will be expressed not in a monastery or in a religious community, but at home and in the workplace. I invite you to adopt this Rule either individually or with others: your spouse, your family, a group of friends, the members of your parish, or some companions in the branch of the Vincentian Family that you belong to.

A Rule is the fruit of experience. It distills the wisdom of those who have gone before us. It is not an abstract document, spinning out a theory about how to live well. Rather, it maps out a path to holiness that many have already trod. It aims to teach a well-tested way of loving. As you read this Rule, think of the wonderful people who have walked before us in our Family: Vincent de Paul, Louise de Marillac, Rosalie Rendu, Frederic Ozanam, Catherine Labouré, Justin De Jacobis, Elisabeth A. Seton, the martyrs in France and Spain and China, and so many others.

Some may be wary of rules. Others may even rebel against them. But in the end, every thoughtful person formulates some kind of rule of life, even if it remains largely unconscious. The goal of a Rule is not to regiment our lives, but rather to create an environment where we can express what is best within us. So I encourage you to think of this Rule not as a series of norms but as a spiritual way. A

Rule is more wisdom than law. Recall the countless lay men and women who have walked before you in the way of the Lord, like Paul's companions Priscilla and Aquila, a married couple who founded the Church at Ephesus and to whom all the Gentile communities were indebted (Rom 16:4). Every reader has known saints – some canonized, most not – people whose lives radiated holiness because the love of God and the love of others, especially the poor, pulsated within them. They concretized the living out of the scriptures through practices like those described in this Rule.

But practices in themselves have only limited value. Through them, a Rule is meant to set us free to love. Love is not the human heart's only response. The heart is also capable of hating, fearing, brooding, resenting, and contemplating revenge. This Rule says: turn everything to love. For that reason, it wants to create a free and open space in your life where the loving presence of God will touch you, because the fundamental mystery of Christianity is not so much that we love God but that God first loves us. So the first space that this Rule aims to hollow out is a sacred dwelling place within you. Over its door is engraved the title "Given to God in Baptism." It is a space not so much to love God as to be loved by God.

This Rule also wants to create a second sacred space in your life, not completely distinct from the first, where the title over the door reads "In the Service of

Others, especially the Poor." It urges you to discipline your heart, your mind, and your use of time and energy, so that you can walk with Jesus as a servant of others, focusing on the neediest among us. Its aim is to liberate you, so that in accepting God's love you might love others practically in return. For that reason, the Rule recalls again and again that the union of prayer and action is the key to genuine holiness.

Of course, a Rule for members of the Vincentian Family cannot be a document aimed at fostering merely individual spiritual heroism. A human community, already graced, is the place of our encounter with God. It is also the matrix of our service of others. So this Rule seeks to create a third sacred space, a place in your life for listening to others, for gathering with them around the Eucharistic table, for supporting them in daily prayer, and for walking with them through life. It calls you, within the context of the worldwide church, to create a "domestic church," a household of faith where family members love one another deeply, where they talk, pray, and plan together, and where they channel their common energies in creative, practical service to others.

It is no surprise that this Rule often holds up Mary the Mother of Jesus as a model of this spiritual way. She, more than any other, created space for God in her life and she let her whole being be transformed by God's expansive love. She is the model listener and the model pray-er. If Christ is the Rule for all of us, then Mary is the preeminent example of how that Rule should be lived.

The authors of ancient and modern Rules often borrowed shamelessly from one another. This Rule is no exception. It says little that is new, but passes on to you the practices and wise advice of holy men and women who have gone before you in the Vincentian Family seeking to follow Christ faithfully. May God, who has begun the same work in you, bring it to fulfillment.

FOCUSING ON CHRIST AS
THE CENTER

*May Christ dwell in your hearts through
faith, so that, being rooted and grounded in
love, you may be able to comprehend with
all the saints what is the breadth and length
and height and depth, and knowing the love
of Christ which surpasses all knowledge,
you may be filled with the fullness of God.*

Ephesians 3:17

*Let us walk with confidence on this royal
road on which Jesus Christ will be our
mentor and guide.*

SV XI, 52

Christ is the absolute center. He is the Rule, as
St. Vincent often said. This seems so obvious, but
nothing is more important. At home with the family,
at work with colleagues, at school, in the parish, or
anywhere else, the lay member of the Vincentian
Family aims to "put on the Lord Jesus Christ" (Rom
13:14). "I am the way, the truth, and the life," Jesus
says, "no one comes to the Father except through
me." "I am the gate." "I am the shepherd." "I am the

light." "I am the vine." "I am the true bread come down from heaven. The one who feeds on my flesh and drinks my blood will live forever."[2]

The Risen Lord has broken through the limits of time and place. He asks followers in every era to learn from him: that he comes from the Father and goes to the Father, that he speaks the truth with courage and love, that he is gentle and humble of heart, that he calls us his friends, that he brings good news especially to the poor and sick, to the broken-hearted and sinners, to prisoners and captive peoples, and that he is faithful even unto death.

Following Christ does not mean copying his life literally. The life-circumstances of a 21st-century Catholic are quite different from those of a 1st-century Jew. While some practices from Jesus' time and place can be transposed to ours, others cannot. The living Church, the community of believers gathered in the Lord's name and confirmed in faith by the pope and the college of bishops, will strengthen you in interpreting the Word of God in today's context.

Christ is present to you in many ways: especially in his word, in the Eucharist, in the community that forms his body, and in the suffering members whom he calls his brothers and sisters.

---

[2] C.f. Jn 14:6, 10:7, 10:11, 8:12, 15:1, 6:41, respectively.

By his preaching and his actions, Christ will teach you what love is. "The way we came to know love was that he laid down his life for us; so we ought to lay down our lives for our brothers" (1 Jn 3:16). So, be converted to love each day.

With Christ, you are called to take the road to Jerusalem, the city of suffering and glorification. As you journey, know that the Lord himself accompanies you. Listen to his words as he speaks with you. Recognize that you are called to serve and not to be served. Help others bear their burdens. Share your goods with the needy.

During the journey, "keep [your] eyes fixed on Jesus, the leader and perfecter of faith. For the sake of the joy that lay before him he endured the cross, despising its shame, and has taken his seat at the right of the throne of God" (Heb 12:2). Do not hesitate to go where he leads you. Do not look back, nor stay where you are. Look to the future with confidence in the Lord.

The chapters that follow propose to you a way of focusing on Christ. Most of all, they call you to listen to him as the Word of God and allow him to penetrate your mind and heart. Christ's way of seeing, feeling, thinking, judging, and acting is to become your way.

As a help in focusing on Christ throughout the day:

- Meditate for ten minutes each morning on the person or the words of Christ as found in the Scriptures.

- Or, meditate before an icon, focusing on the compassion of Jesus.

- Carry away a word or a phrase from your meditation and repeat it reflectively at quiet moments during the day, such as while waiting in line or riding in the car.

- As an alternative, repeat the "Jesus Prayer" often throughout the day: "Lord Jesus Christ, Son of God, have mercy on me, a sinner."

- Strive to see Christ in the vulnerable and the marginalized. Reach out to him in them through some practical form of service, whether direct or indirect. Recall that the needy you serve are your brothers and sisters with whom Christ identifies. Be conscious that the Church, in order to be faithful, must have a special bond with the poor.

LISTENING TO THE WORD OF GOD

Each morning he awakes me to hear to listen like a disciple. The Lord Yahweh has opened my ear.

Is 50:4-5

Each one must strive, above all else, to ground himself in this truth: the teaching of Christ can never deceive, while that of the world is always false, since Christ himself declares that the latter is like a house built upon sand, whereas he compares his own to a building founded upon solid rock.

CR II, 1

As a disciple, the first service that you owe God is to listen. In Jesus' time, all faithful Jews memorized the stirring words of Deuteronomy (6:4-7): "Hear, O Israel! The Lord is our God, the Lord alone! Therefore, you shall love the Lord, your God, with all your heart, and with all your soul, and with all your strength. Take to heart these words which I enjoin on you today. Drill them into your children.

Speak of them at home and abroad, whether you are busy or at rest."

Love of God begins with listening to God's word and believing in God's love for us: "In this is love: not that we have loved God, but that he loved us" (1 John 4:10). So also will your love for the neighbor begin with listening.

Learn, then, to be a good listener. Allow yourself to be informed, taught, and changed by others as they "preach the gospel" through what they do and say – by the members of your family, by those you work with, and especially by the poor. You must first hear the good news before you can respond to it and live it.

As you listen, the word of God will enter your life in strikingly diverse ways. It will change you. Sometimes it will come as food (Ps 19:11) to strengthen you and build you up. Sometimes it will be refreshing water (Is 55:10) to quench your thirst on the journey. At other times God's word will jolt you like a hammer that shatters a rock (Jer 23:29), breaking in on your too-settled ways or your hardness of heart. It may also strike you like a two-edged sword (Heb 4:12) to pierce your resistance.

Read a portion of the scriptures meditatively each day. St. Vincent tells us that the word of God never fails. It is deeply personal. It is addressed not only to the whole community of believers, but to you as an individual. Listen to it, meditate on it, digest it, and act on it. You will then be like "a house built upon rock." In practice, as a means of reflecting on the scriptures daily, some meditate on the readings the church chooses for the mass that day. Others adopt a systematic way of reading the entire Bible each year.

In the scriptures God often complains that, though he speaks, his people "do not listen." The true prophets were pre-eminent listeners; they heard what God had to say and then spoke in God's name. "Speak, Lord, for your servant is listening," said the boy Samuel (1 Sam 3:10) as he began his prophetic career.

We believe that Jesus is the Word of God, the fulfillment of the scriptures. In him the new and everlasting covenant between God and God's people has been definitively forged. Jesus' person and his words reveal God to us.

Mary is the preeminent disciple. She listens to God's word and puts it into practice. When the angel Gabriel speaks to her, she responds wholeheartedly: "Be it done to me according to your word" (Lk 1:38).

Joseph reacts similarly. Four angelic messengers speak to him. As soon as he hears what they ask, he gets up immediately and carries out God's command (Mt 2: 14,21).

Those who do likewise will be happy. The gospels assure us that real happiness does not lie in being close to Jesus physically, nor in a blood relationship with him, but in listening to the word of God and acting on it.

While he was speaking, a woman from the crowd called out and said to him, "Happy is the womb that carried you and the breasts at which you nursed." He replied, "Rather, happy are those who hear the word of God and observe it." (Lk 11:27-28)

Listening and humility are closely allied. Those who recognize with humble gratitude that life, truth, wisdom, and love are gifts of God have already made listening their basic attitude.

St. Vincent calls humility the foundation of evangelical perfection and the core of the spiritual life. The humble see everything as gift. They believe that God is always seeking to enter their lives to speak with them. So they are alert, attentive, and eager to hear God's Word. The humble know that the truth which sets them free comes from without: through the scriptures, through the Church, through the members of their family, through the cries of the poor.

Listen, then, to your family. Listen to those at work. Listen to the Word of God each day, choosing a small portion of the scriptures as food to nourish your prayer.

Listening is especially important when you exercise authority, as do parents, teachers, doctors, nurses, or bosses. When you hold authority, be sure to seek wise counsel often. Take advice. There is no room for arrogance in the following of Christ.

The opening words of the Rule of Saint Benedict are fundamental for all who wish to learn from the Lord: "Listen carefully to the master's instructions, and attend to them with the ear of your heart."

As a help in listening:

- When you pray, relax and breathe deeply. Begin simply and peacefully. Let sounds, thoughts, and anxieties subside. Be quiet. Seek to hear the word of God.

- Take a few minutes each day to sit and listen to your spouse, child, friend, a co-worker or a poor person. Be attentive as they narrate an event of their day, a problem, a concern or a joy. Listen without interjecting comments, advice, or judgment. Focus entirely on the other person.

LOVING AT HOME

Put on then, as God's chosen ones, holy and beloved, heartfelt compassion, kindness, humility, gentleness, and patience, bearing with one another and forgiving one another, if one has a grievance against another; as the Lord has forgiven you, so must you also do. And over all these put on love, that is, the bond of perfection.

Col 3:12-14

Gentleness! Gentleness! Oh, what a beautiful virtue! Gentleness and Humility are two twin sisters who get along well together and who, like Simplicity and Prudence, can never be separated.

SV XII, 184

God calls most men and women to marry, to make a covenant with their spouse to work out their holiness together. Married couples pledge to love one another as Christ loved the Church, with a love that is sacrificial, forgiving, service-oriented, and faithful unto death. By their lives they witness to the

Trinitarian revelation that God is communion and that we discover God whenever and wherever we give ourselves over to communion.

Over the centuries, many husbands and wives from all strata of society have become saints. Some have been canonized; most have not. At the head of the list stand Mary and Joseph, who supported their family from the earnings of a wood-worker's shop. Priscilla and Aquila, the founders of the Church of Ephesus, labored as tent- makers. Justinian (482-565) and Theodora, saints in the Orthodox tradition, served as emperor and empress. Isidore of Madrid and María de la Cabeza (12th century) toiled as farmers. Countless other married couples, never canonized, have followed these saints on the road to holiness. Such saintly couples have abounded in our Vincentian Family. Three of the founders of our largest branches – Louise de Marillac, Elizabeth Ann Seton, and Frederic Ozanam – were married and loved their spouses deeply. Numerous husbands and wives in our Family serve the poor generously today.

Married life is the vocation in which most Christians grow holy or fail to do so. Ironically, some spouses become saints *in spite of* their husband or wife, or precisely *because of* the difficulties created by their partner, but that is by no means the Christian ideal. The ideal is that a husband and wife walk the Christian journey together. Their pilgrimage is a joint project, though ultimately neither husband nor wife can shirk personal responsibility for responding to God's gift of holiness.

Couples should often recall the beautiful name that Vatican II used when it described the family as "the domestic Church."[3] Like the Church, the family is a community in which the gospel is handed on, from spouse to spouse and from parents to children. From them it radiates out to others by the household's example of unity and love.

Daily life is the stuff of which holiness is made. A husband and wife will enrich their marriage by:

- being genuine lovers living together in intimate friendship

- communicating well between themselves and with their children

- being sensitive to each other's emotional, physical, and spiritual needs and learning how to express their love in ways that will meet those needs

- recognizing their own human weakness as well as their spouse's and helping one another to grow

---

3 Lumen Gentium 11; Apostolicam Actuositatem, 11.

- forgiving and being reconciled, even on a daily basis

- dealing with conflicts promptly through humble dialogue rather than defensive argumentation

- valuing the differences God has given to them and learning how to capitalize on those differences to make their marriage fruitful

- managing their household and its finances in a way that minimizes stress.

A family meal, eaten together daily, can be a rich time of communication and presence to one another. It is important for parents and children, whenever possible, to arrange their schedules to join in a family meal rather than let life's other demands continually dictate when and how they eat. In the spirit of the gospels, the family should begin that meal with a prayer invoking the Lord's blessing and recalling the Eucharistic meal that binds us together. There are many such prayers, such as: "God, the Father of mercies, you willed that your Son would take flesh in order to give life back to us. Bless + these your gifts with which we are about to nourish our bodies, so that, receiving new strength, we may wait in watchfulness for the glorious coming of Christ. We ask this in his name. R. Amen."

Occasionally, it will be helpful for parents to eat by themselves and dialogue about their life together in an atmosphere of trusting love.

In conjunction with their other obligations, all in the family can share in chores like cooking, washing dishes, cleaning, and other household work.

Prayer together as a family at some time each day will enrich the lives of spouses and will also teach their children to pray. Families might wish to pray the rosary together, or a psalm like Ps. 91, or simply an Our Father or Hail Mary. The members of the family can help one another to learn to pray not only at times of formal prayer, but also in free quiet moments, like times of waiting or driving in the car or traveling by train or air.

Time together is a treasure that families can easily lose if members become too absorbed in their work, or if they give too much time to television, the phone or the computer. Turning off TVs and cell phones as a family eats and converses can be a blessing for all.

Healthy families have fun and find occasions for going out together, vacationing as a family, and enjoying one another's company.

Hobbies enrich a family's life. Activities like walking or other forms of exercise, reading, listening to music, and seeing films together provide diversion, enjoyment, and interesting conversation. Loving parents will often accompany children as they participate in sports, scouts, plays, and other events.

In a society characterized by individualism, it is crucial to foster family unity by preserving traditional ways and inventing new ways of handing on to future generations a capacity for living together in love. The family itself is a school of practical love where members learn to care for elderly grandparents, a sick child, or a troubled brother or sister, and where they seek to heal brokenness.

Lay members of the Vincentian Family will live, pray and serve others not only in their own "domestic church," but also in a local church and in the universal church. Aware of their membership in a universal church, they will develop a global point of view. They will be conscious that the ocean's waves break on other shores where many of the world's poorest people – women, children, and refugees – live and labor. This will help them to be creative in finding ways to assist the neediest.

Pope John Paul II presented us with an eloquent challenge: "The century and the millennium now beginning will need to see ... to what length of dedication the Christian community can go in charity toward the poorest. If we have truly started out afresh from the contemplation of Christ, we must learn to see him especially in the face of those with whom he himself wished to be identified: 'I was hungry and you gave me food, I was thirsty and you gave me drink...' (Mt 25:35ff). This gospel text is not a simple invitation to charity: it is a page of Christology which sheds a ray of light on the mystery of Christ."[4]

Families can respond to this challenge together by their volunteering as a group at a center for senior citizens, for example, or at a shelter for the homeless, or by caring for a home-bound neighbor. A family's care for others in need is a way of sharing the gifts that God has given it. In such a context, life at home can be a genuine "school of service" for the young.

---

[4] Novo Millennio Ineunte (NMI, 49).

LIVING THE SINGLE VOCATION

As each one has received a gift, use it to serve one another as good stewards of God's varied grace.

1 Peter 4:10

The Kingdom of God is peace in the Holy Spirit. God will reign in you if your heart is at peace.

SV I, 114

Everyone lives out a significant portion of life as a single young man or woman, seeking the Lord in that state and attempting to discern what direction to take in an uncertain future. Some choose to remain single for life. Others stay single for a considerable time as they search for a marriage partner; this period is often quite lengthy, since the age at which young people marry is now rising in most parts of the world. Still others continue in the single state not by inclination, but because of a variety of circumstances, sometimes freely chosen or sometimes quite unwanted. And still others marry but become single again because of the death of a spouse or a broken marriage.

Today we speak too of "single parents," though in fact their vocation is different from that of those who remain completely single and it shares aspects of both the married and the single life.

The single vocation has its beauty and its burdens. Like all vocations, it is not an end in itself, but a way of self-giving.

Its beauty lies in the unique opportunities it offers. It allows abundant time, freedom, and flexibility to explore multiple possibilities for giving oneself in the service of others. The single person is mobile, since he or she has not established a fixed bond with a community of persons, as those who are married do. For that reason, the single vocation demands careful, ongoing discernment about how to give one's life.

The single also have the opportunity for considerable solitude, especially if they live alone. This solitude invites them to focus on God in prayer.

But like all vocations, the single life has its burdens. Loneliness is one of them. The challenge for the single is to find healthy ways of moving beyond loneliness to self-giving involvement with others. Since they will not be generating new life in children, it is crucial that those who choose the single state know how they will generate life and how they will hand on God's gifts to those around them. The possibilities are many: teaching, the healing professions, artistic contributions, research, writing, direct service of those in need.

A second burden is the lack of a built-in support system. This vacuum challenges the single person to build friendships that will contribute to a healthy environment for growth. While friends are important for everyone, they are all the more important for the single. The various lay branches of our Vincentian Family can offer friendship and support to the single, whether young, middle-aged, or older.

It is imperative that those who are single because of unwanted circumstances or a broken relationship avoid bitterness and alienation. Jesus assures us that God provides, even in trying times. He encourages us to pray for those who have hurt us. As we ask God's blessing on them, the healing blessing of the Lord will descend upon us. We are truly blessed when love and forgiveness supplant hostility and anger.

The single young person, as he or she moves from childhood to adolescence to adulthood, has unique opportunities and faces significant challenges.

Youth is a time of learning. It has a remarkable plasticity about it. The life of the young changes quickly and at times dramatically. The positive side of this plasticity is youth's capacity to adjust, be formed, and grow.

Young people long to know how to love. The search for significant relationships occupies a huge space on their agenda. At the same time, many are drawn toward transcendence. They begin to yearn for a love that goes beyond their everyday experience of love.

A synod of the world's bishops wrote this rousing message to the young:

You, young people, you are "sentinels of the morning." ... How is the Lord of history asking you to build a civilization of love? You have a keen sense of what honesty and sincerity require ... How can we be disciples of Jesus together and put into practice Christ's teaching on the Mount of the Beatitudes? [5]

The Church calls the young to sing a wake-up song in the world, as did the sentinel in the ancient world who stood on the city wall eager to catch the first glimpse of the rising sun and proclaim its arrival. Of course, in a Christian worldview, the rising sun whom we proclaim is Jesus, the Risen Lord. Our Vincentian Family's youth groups will offer the young a gradually deepening formation

---

[5] 10th Ordinary General Assembly of the Synod of Bishops. September 30 – October 27, 2001.

in the following of Christ, friendship and support in doing so, and concrete opportunities to serve Christ in the person of the poor.

Young people, in their formative years in their family, at school or with their peers, should seek to be deeply confident in the presence of the Risen Lord and develop a profoundly gospel-centered spirituality. This is especially possible in a family whose members have that same confidence in the Lord and support one another in living his life.

In their later years, many who had once been married find themselves single again. Ideally, peaceful serenity, joyful confidence, ongoing conversion, and frequent prayer will characterize this final single stage of life. Of course, the evangelical challenge is to continue to grow in practical, outgoing love. Here too our Vincentian lay associations can offer rich opportunities.

It is wonderful to see aging people who continue to be creative and retain a young heart. For single aging people, the later years offer a special opportunity to develop the contemplative and service dimensions of their person. It is also a time for reconciliation with the past, for healing wounds, for letting go of unrealized dreams, and for assessing the reality of their life.

The word "single" means "unique;" it also means "alone." The single life is unique because it is not easily categorized; it allows for multiple possibilities for the gift of oneself. "Single" means "alone" in the sense that, whether by choice or by circumstance, the single walk in the way of the Lord without a spouse. Prayerful intimacy with the Lord will help heal the pain of aloneness and make the single life fertile and deep.

In living out their vocation, it is especially helpful for those who choose the single state:

- to maintain a discerning posture throughout life, from their initial search for a career as a young person, through a service-oriented adulthood, and into the later years when they enjoy freer moments and have new choices to make

- to develop a sense of their unique personal vocation and the ways in which the Lord calls them to give

- to focus generously on practical, effective service, directing their time and talents toward the needy around them

- to nourish the contemplative dimension of life, taking time for quiet prayer, avoiding the temptation to flee from loneliness through long hours of watching TV, surfing the web, or employing other time-killers that have limited, or even negative, value

- to form healthy friendships that will provide human support and strengthen their life in the Lord.

Serviens in spe

SERVING IN THE WORKPLACE

I am among you as one who serves.

Lk 22:27

There is no better way to assure our eternal happiness than to live and die in the service of the poor, within the arms of Providence, and in a real renunciation of ourselves by following Jesus Christ.

SV III, 392

Spouses, children, teachers, students, doctors, nurses, lawyers, manual laborers – all are called to build their lives on the gospel mandate to serve. Gospel service can be as simple as "giving a cup of cold water" (Mt 10:42) to the thirsty. From the prominent politician who regards himself as a public servant, to the obscure poor person who finds ways of helping those who are even poorer – all must embrace in his or her way Jesus' servant role.

Jesus radiates joy as a servant. He tells us that "there is more happiness in giving than in receiving" (Acts 20:35). In the Vincentian Family, we rejoice to be servants of the poor, "our lords and masters." As servants, we strive, in the footsteps of Christ, to keep our own needs few, to be grateful to

God for what we have, to be generous with our possessions, and to ask for little beyond God's love.

Our service will shape us. Work develops the worker. It plays a very important role in everyone's life. It is not for amassing, but for giving. Though it will often be a burden, and sometimes a cross, through it we co-create with God. As servants we are called to work hard. That is the normal lot of a servant. Since, in our Vincentian Family, service occupies such a significant portion of our time, the choice of what we do requires considerable discernment.

Time is a gift to be treasured. It is easy to fritter it away in useless matters, like idle gossip. St. Vincent urges us to use our time well.

Outgoing charity is the core of following Christ. "This is how all will know that you are my disciples, if you have love for one another" (Jn 13:35). Regard yourself as being at the beck and call of "the least of my brothers and sisters."

Jesus continually reminds leaders that they are members of a servant church. "If anyone wishes to be first", he tells his followers, "he shall be the last of all and the servant of all" (Mr 9:35). Those in leadership, whether in the workplace or in the political arena or elsewhere, are called to exercise authority humbly and to work at creating just living and working conditions among those they serve.

Catholic social teaching, proclaimed so eloquently but often so little-known, focuses especially on the neediest in society. It is the foundation for the Church's "preferential option for the poor." Awareness of that tradition will help us to see the world and the poor with Jesus' eyes.

St. Vincent told his followers that the poor are the real royalty in the Church. In the world of faith, the neediest are the kings and queens; we are their servants. It is they especially whom we listen to and obey.

Your love of the needy will often go unrequited. You will meet frustrations, complaints, and criticisms when serving others. But if you persevere with a love that manifests joy, enthusiasm, and generosity, you grow deeper in Jesus' life.

St. Vincent and many other saints learned this rule from the Lord: first, do; then, teach:

1) through the language of works: performing the works of justice and mercy – which are a sign that the Kingdom of God is really alive among us – such as feeding the hungry, giving drink to the thirsty, helping to find the causes of their hunger and thirst and the ways of alleviating them, giving to charities that serve the immediate needs of the poor, contributing to organizations that work to change structures and help the disadvantaged emerge from poverty;

2) through the language of words: speaking sincerely and truthfully; assuring others that your prayers are with them, and meaning it; announcing with deep conviction the Lord's presence, his love, his offer of forgiveness and his acceptance of all;

3) through the language of relationships: being with the poor, working with them, forming a community with them that shows the Lord's love for each individual; developing genuine personal bonds based on respect for the personal dignity of others.

The spirituality of our Family places great emphasis on the concrete, the practical. "Let us love God, let us love God," St. Vincent reminds his followers, "but let it be with the strength of our arms and the sweat of our brow" (SV XI, 40). But St. Vincent also teaches us that the key to perseverance in serving others lovingly is the ability to combine action and prayer, recognizing humbly that God is the source of all good.

As members of a Family, we serve with others. We unite our gifts in the service of God and in the service of the poor. We work and pray, plan and evaluate together. We organize projects among the needy, with each one contributing his or her talents. We invite others to join us in attending to the marginalized, thus multiplying our forces as a Family that focuses on the poor.

By the very fact that your vocation is lay, you have a special role to play in evangelizing the world of culture, politics, economics, the sciences, the arts, civil society, and the media.

Today lay men and women are also called to exercise a very wide variety of ministries within the Church: as heads of local Church communities, both small and large; as catechists, teachers, directors of prayer; as leaders of services of the Word of God; as ministers to the sick in their homes and in hospitals; and as servants of the poor. In the future, even more than at present, lay people will serve in parish planning and administration, animating prayer through song and art, setting up web sites on Internet, and evangelizing in countless other ways, both directly and indirectly.

As a lay member of the Vincentian Family in the 21st century you are called to be not just well-educated in a secular field, but well formed in faith. In fact, faith-formation is crucial for growth in God's life. Lay members of our Family will receive formation first in their homes, then also in Catholic schools, in parish religious education programs, and in youth groups. In an ongoing way throughout their lives, the reading of materials like Catholic newspapers, books, periodicals, and websites will keep them well-informed and will nourish their faith.

A danger in the lives of all servants is activism. If the contemplative might try to live like an angel, the servant might try to live like a messiah, shouldering all the world's problems. If the former does too little, the latter attempts too much, burning himself or herself out and winding up not just overworked and over-stimulated, but disillusioned and bitter. St. Vincent called this "indiscreet zeal" (SV I, 84).

God calls us not just to work, but to rest. In fact, God commands us to rest (Ex 20:8, Ps 127:2). In a world that is frenetic at times, it is important that we learn to rest and that we develop good leisure habits, like reading, physical exercise, and the enjoyment of art and music.

ROOTING LIFE IN PRAYER

Then he told them a parable about the necessity for them to pray always without becoming weary.

Luke 18:1

Give me a man of prayer and he will be capable of everything. He may say with the Apostle, "I can do all things in Him who strengthens me."

SV XI, 83

Jesus' prayer leaps off the pages of the gospels. Christians have always been fascinated by his union with God, whom he called his Father. His disciples asked him to teach them to pray (Lk 11:1). Jesus' reply is addressed to every reader of the gospels: "When you pray, say: Our Father…" (Lk 11:2).

Jesus teaches us to use diverse forms of prayer. He praises and thanks God, he expresses fear and anxiety, he asks forgiveness for his enemies. His emphasis on prayer of petition is striking: "If [the] wicked know how to give good gifts to [their] children, how much more will the Father in heaven give the holy Spirit to those who ask him?" (Lk 11:13).

Throughout history, faithful followers of Jesus have consistently recognized the need for union with God in prayer. From the earliest times, Christians prayed daily in their homes and gathered in "domestic churches" for the breaking of the bread. Later, courageous men and women went off into the desert to pray in imitation of Jesus, and gradually formed communities dedicated to prayer. As they prayed, disciples sought to hear the deepest voices of reality in the word of God and the cries of suffering humanity.

Among the many prayer forms that are possible in a lay person's life, I encourage you to embrace especially those that follow.

Participate actively with others at the Sunday Eucharist as a privileged time with the Lord. Teach and encourage your whole family to do so. If the priest preaches well during the celebration, thank the Lord for this gift and put God's Word into practice. If he preaches poorly, try all the harder to discern what the Word of God is asking of you that day.

Spend at least ten minutes each day with the Lord in silent, meditative prayer. This is not an easy commitment to keep in the midst of a busy schedule at home or at work or at school, but, I assure you, it will slowly change your life. Find a place where, in the words of Matthew's gospel, you can shut the door on the noise of the world. There, listen well and speak with the Lord simply. Read a small passage from the scriptures, if you should like, and ask the Lord, "Lord, what are you saying to me? What do you want me to do today?"

Pray briefly with your family before your main meal. Eat that meal together each day as often as possible. Let it be a time of genuine communication and sharing. Let your prayer echo some of the beautiful meal prayers handed down in the Judaeo-Christian tradition, such as: "Praise be to you, our God, Creator of time and space, you who in your goodness feed the entire world. With kindness and graciousness you give bread to every creature, for your loving kindness is unending. Great is the glory of your name, for you, our God, feed the world, bringing goodness to all, preparing food for all your creatures. Praise be to you who feed the world."

Kneel at your bedside or sit in a quiet place to pray in the morning and in the evening, even if only for a short time. Some find journaling at the end of the day a helpful means for growing in the Lord's life and in gratitude for God's gifts. Some use icons to help them focus as they pray. Some light candles. Some play quiet music. Some pray as they drive, shutting off the radio and the CD player, or playing gentle music in the background. Some pray while they walk or stand in line waiting. In prayer, there are many ways, fitting different personalities.

In the morning, dedicate the day to the Lord, asking God's blessing on its main events. The saints offer us many striking prayers well suited for the morning, like that of St. Ignatius:

Take, Lord, and receive all my liberty, my memory, my understanding, and my entire will, all that I have and call my own. You have given all to me. To you, Lord, I return it. All is yours. Dispose of it wholly according to your will. Give me only your love and grace. That is enough for me.

Night is a time for quiet and for peaceful sleep. Before retiring, make a brief examination of conscience. Look back over the day. Ask yourself: When did I love? When did I fail? What patterns do I see in my life? Notice both the positive and the negative, the lights and the shadows. Thank the Lord for the day's gifts and ask pardon and healing for your failures. Commend yourself to the Lord, placing your life in his hands. A long tradition in the Church ends the day with a Marian prayer, like the "Hail, Holy Queen."

Occasionally, when the opportunity arises, take part in a parish mission or in a retreat with the members of our Vincentian Family as a time for reflection and growth.

It is important for spouses to seek an occasional quiet time when they are alone and can dialogue prayerfully about how their life together is going.

Fidelity in prayer demands personal discipline. Just as constancy in exercising trains the athlete, the musician, and the dancer for the art they practice, so also faithfulness in setting aside time and entering a quiet space enable the pray-er to stand before the Lord each day and say "Speak, Lord, for your servant is listening."

Even prayer has its dangers. Two extremes should be avoided.

The first is "escapism," which draws us to flee from life's anguishing problems and seek refuge in passive solitude. Prayer, on the contrary, should immerse us in life and enable us to hear reality's deepest voices. If we simply escape from life, we will remain rapt in isolation and will have little interest in the real needs of others.

The second is "angelism", or an overly spiritual approach to life. Those who pray genuinely are steeped in life's concreteness. Real Christian love bodies forth in acts. A person is surely suspect who has beautiful contemplative moments but who does little or is difficult to relate to. "By their fruits you shall know them" (Mt 7:16). A great Russian author once wrote: "Love in practice is a harsh and dreadful thing compared with love in dreams." [6]

---

[6] Fydor Dostoevsky. The Brothers Karamazov. Part I, book 2, chapter 4, pg. 61. (New York, NY: Spark Publishing: 2004)

JOURNEYING WITH FRIENDS

A faithful friend is a sturdy shelter.
Whoever finds one finds a treasure.

Sirach 6:14

Care for one another as friends who love
each other deeply

CR VIII, 2

Friendship has a privileged place in the Judeo-Christian tradition. "God is friendship," wrote St. Aelred of Rievaulx. The scriptures tell us of God's intimate relationship with Abraham, Moses, David, and many others. In the Book of Exodus, when Moses prays, God answers: "This request, too, which you have just made, I will carry out, because you have found favor with me and you are my intimate friend" (Ex 33:17).

Likewise the New Testament speaks of the close bonds that Jesus forges with a number of his followers. John states unambiguously: "Jesus loved Martha, and her sister and Lazarus" (Jn 11:5). So too, the gospels leave little doubt about Jesus' friendship with Mary Magdalene and other women. At the end of his life, Jesus tells those gathered around him at the Last Supper that they are no longer servants but his friends (Jn 15:15). He shares with them "everything I have heard from my Father."

Friends of the Lord are called to be each others' friends. In fact, the New Testament model for human friendship is Jesus' friendship with us: "Love one another as I love you. No one has greater love than this, to lay down one's life for one's friends" (Jn 15:12-13). That is surely a very demanding standard.

Friends accompany us on life's journey. Intimate, long-lived, mature friendships are different from simple camaraderie. Genuine friends touch something deep within us. Such friendships are very varied. They sometimes arise between people of different ages and different sexes. They sometimes develop slowly between spouses, brothers and sisters, parents and children. The scriptures sing the praises of faithful friendships. Ben Sirach tells us: "A faithful friend is beyond price, no sum can balance his worth" (Sir 6:15).

Genuine friends respect our deepest values and support us in our commitment to live the gospel. They strengthen us in fidelity to our vocation in life rather than distracting us from it. Within our Vincentian Family, we form bonds of friendship and support one another in following Christ and in serving the poor.

Friends are surely one of life's greatest gifts. Some of the signs of the joyful, healthy, loving relationship that we call friendship are these:

- **It involves deep mutual resonance** – Friendship is intimate. Philosophers sometimes describe it as "a single soul in two bodies" or speak of a friend as "a second self." The Book of Samuel depicts the remarkable relationship between David and Jonathan in these words: "Jonathan had become as fond of David as if his life depended on him; he loved him as he loved himself" (1 Sam 18:1). It says that David's love for Jonathan was stronger even than married love (2 Sam 1:26).

- **It thrives on open communication** – Opening one's heart is the key to friendship. Friends speak freely with one another. They share each other's joys and sorrows, hopes and fears. Sometimes their mutual knowledge is quite intuitive, so that they sense, long before words are spoken, that a wonderful event is about to occur or that something painful has happened.

- **It brings out positive traits in us** – There is something in each of us that only friends can bring out fully. In the gospel narratives Jesus calls forth a hidden beauty from within Mary Magdalene. He encourages and nourishes a contemplative dimension in Mary, the sister of Martha and Lazarus.

- **It is resilient** – Even good friends hurt each other at times. No friendship is without its ups and downs. Thoughtless words slip out at times. Work or other activities sometimes lead us to neglect those we care for most. It is very important that we keep our friendships in good repair. But because genuine friendships are solid, they do not easily break. Friends bounce back from setbacks and reestablish the mutual confidence that may for a time have been damaged.

- **It is enduring** – Christian tradition assures us that friendship, like all love, is abiding. It breaks even the bonds of death. We continue to love deceased friends. The author of Hebrews encourages us with the image of the "great cloud of witnesses" (Heb 12:1) that surrounds us. Christian creeds profess that we believe in the "communion of saints." How many Christians through the centuries have loved Mary the mother of Jesus and sensed her love for them. How many have had special saints with whom they could speak confidently about their daily cares and needs. How many have believed deeply in the abiding presence of those who have "gone before us marked with the sign of faith:" parents, brothers and sisters, close friends, who surround us as we celebrate the Eucharist and are there encouraging us as we pour out our hearts in silent prayer.

- **It is free** – We choose our friends freely. The challenge is to choose them well. Experience teaches that we become like our friends, for better or for worse. Parents instinctively become alarmed when their children keep bad company because they know that we breathe the air that surrounds us and absorb both its beneficial and malignant contents.

- **It involves laughter and fun as well as sorrow and pain** – Friends enjoy each other's company. They forge a bond that brings good humor to life, even sometimes in its darker moments. We can count on friends both in good times and in bad. A faithful friend knows how to "rejoice with those who rejoice, weep with those who weep" (Rom 12:15).

St. Vincent tells us that friendship will unite our hearts and actions, not only among ourselves but with Our Lord, and that, consequently, friendship will bring us great peace (SV VI, 46). He prays for the members of the Family he founded: "May it please God to unite all of you very closely with an indissoluble bond of charity, so that by your mutual friendship, others will recognize you as true children of Our Lord… I ask the Holy Spirit, who is the union of the Father and the Son, to give you this grace" (SV V, 64).

It is normal for us to have friends of both sexes. In fact, it is important that we develop good, open-ended relationships with both men and women. This is true for married people as well as for those who are single. But there is a perennial wisdom that can be applied even to the most positive friendships between men and women: not just any time, or place, or circumstance is appropriate for relationships. While it is difficult to draw up precise rules in this regard, it is imperative that we know our own limitations and that we be disciplined enough to live within their bounds.

Few things are more important on life's journey than a wise "soul friend." As a picturesque Celtic saying puts it, "Anyone without a soul friend is a body without a head." It is especially useful to speak with a soul friend about our prayer, our relationships, our service to the poor, our intense feelings, our joys and sorrows, our problems. Speaking honestly about our inner struggles, even if we find ourselves embarrassed about them, can be a wonderful relief and a first step toward integration and healing. Of course, it is imperative that we choose "soul friends" well. An immature guide can be worse than none at all. A "soul friend" should be a wise, experienced person of deep faith.

HAVING A GRATEFUL HEART

My soul proclaims the greatness of the Lord; My spirit rejoices in God my savior. For he has looked upon his handmaid's lowliness; Behold, from now on will all ages call me blessed.
The Mighty One has done great things for me, and holy is his name.

Luke 1:46-49

Ingratitude is the crime of crimes.

SV VIII, 37

Christian prayer is most of all praise and gratitude. I encourage you to learn to pray as Mary did in the Magnificat. This prayer has a special place in Luke's gospel, in the daily prayer of the Church, and in the tradition of our Vincentian Family.

The Magnificat is a freedom song. Mary, the lead singer, represents the lowly of Israel, those marginalized by society, for whom there is no room in the inn (Lk 2:7). God is her only hope, and she sings God's praises with gratitude. She rejoices because she is conscious of how good God has been to her.

Knowing God as mighty, holy, merciful, and faithful to the promises found in the scriptures, she has exuberant confidence. For Mary, nothing is impossible to God. This belief enables her to pray with joy. She believes that God can heal the sick, change the sinner, and overcome even death.

Mary recognizes that God plays no favorites (Lev 19:15), so she trusts that God's power will vindicate the innocent and the oppressed and will undo the plots of evildoers. She sees God as the friend of the widow, the orphan, and the refugee.

Since God is awesome, utterly distinct from all created beings, she stands in God's presence with reverence, or "fear of the Lord." But at the same time, she believes that this awesome God, so set apart from created things, is intimately present to her, drawing her near "with bands of love" (Hos 11:4).

Mary's prayer is very covenant-oriented. God's covenant with Abraham plays a foundational role in her faith as a Jewish woman. She is deeply conscious that she is a member of a chosen people. Now, she believes that God has established a new covenant that far surpasses all previous expectations. She delights that the final era of human history has begun. She sings. She praises. She gives thanks.

Like Mary, pray with gratitude. The word "Eucharist," the sign of the new covenant which we re-enact again and again in memory of Jesus, means "thanksgiving."

From the earliest times, Christians saw the Eucharist as a thanksgiving meal, in continuity with similar Hebrew meals. So, at the beginning of every Eucharistic Prayer, the celebrant and assembly cry out:

Celebrant: *Let us give thanks to the Lord Our God*

Assembly: *It is right to give him thanks and praise*

Celebrant: *Father, All Powerful and Ever-living God, we do well always and everywhere to give you thanks...*

All Eucharistic Prayers express words of gratitude to God the Father, recalling the gifts of creation and redemption. They focus on the love of God's Son, who gave his life for all. They invoke the presence of God's Spirit to sanctify the Eucharistic gifts and those who receive them.

Thanksgiving is an indispensable theme in prayer. Recognizing God's gifts, a believer will radiate gratitude and joy.

As a help toward living and praying with gratitude, seek to develop a Eucharistic attitude:

- Remember events from salvation history as taught in the scriptures, and thank God for them.

- Remember events from your personal history and thank God for them.

- As often as you can during the day, make a point of being aware of God's gifts.

- Give thanks to God for life, health, talents, opportunities, family, friends, coworkers, your contacts and friendships with the poor, your insights, and anything else that you are aware of.

- Be grateful even in the midst of adversity, illness, and personal crises. Be aware that God is with you and give thanks for that abiding presence.

- Say prayers of thanks to God often throughout the day: anything from a simple "Thank you, Lord" to a more formal "Blessed are you God, who…"

- Express your gratitude to others; tell them often of the things you are grateful for.

SPEAKING THE TRUTH

I speak the truth in Christ, I do not lie; my conscience joins with the Holy Spirit in bearing me witness.

Rom 9:1

Simplicity is the virtue I love most. I call it my gospel.

SV I, 284; IX, 606

Making friends, falling in love, building a family, being part of a movement, a community, a nation – all these forms of union with others are possible only if there is truth-filled communication.

For Christians, truth-telling is fundamental. In Matthew's gospel Jesus lays down a basic imperative: "Let your yes mean yes and your no mean no" (Mt. 5:37). The importance of this saying for the early Christian community is evident since two other independent New Testament sources record it (James 5:12; 2 Cor. 1:17-20).

But experience proves that it is very difficult to let our yes mean yes and our no mean no. Lies bring about the disintegration of friendships, the fracture of marriages, even the downfall of governments.

Such lies are not just verbal; they are often acted out. Marriages collapse through infidelity. Friendships unravel through secret betrayal. Families break down through covert, competing interests.

Within the Church, as members of the Vincentian Family, we seek the truth with others. A fundamental means for doing so is to listen humbly to all. Our ears should be open to the words of those who teach officially in the church, like the pope and bishops, but also to the cries of the poor, our brothers and sisters. In fact the latter, who so often go unheard, must have a privileged voice in the Church and in our lives.

Simplicity, or passion for the truth, holds a special place in the Vincentian tradition. St. Vincent held it up as a fundamental virtue for all the groups he founded. He saw it as a mission-oriented virtue that would enable us to identify with the poor and communicate authentically with them.

Growth in truth-telling is a lifelong process. Limited objectives like power, self-promotion, sex, and money easily intrude on our single-minded pursuit of truth. In our sinful condition, we never pull our lives together once and for all as a completed masterpiece. Even those who seem to have it together sometimes falter badly. Final integrity in the truth comes only through God's forgiving, healing love. It is a gift.

John's gospel, especially, highlights the importance of both speaking and living the truth. In the Johannine perspective, Jesus is the truth (4:6). The person who acts in the truth comes into the light (3:21). The truth sets us free (8:32). When the Spirit comes, he will guide us to all truth (16:13). Jesus has come to testify to the truth (18:37). Anyone who is of the truth hears his voice (18:37).

There is a great attractiveness about those who speak the truth. They are truly free. We relate to them easily because we sense that they are transparent and have no hidden agendas.

Yet speaking the truth with consistency is an extremely difficult discipline. We are tempted to blur the truth when our own convenience is at stake or when the truth is embarrassing to us personally.

Nor is it easy to be consistently true to one's word, one's promises, and one's commitments. Truth, in this sense, is fidelity. It is in this sense especially that Jesus is true to us. He promises to be, and is, with us always, even to the end. In this same sense we are called to be true to friendships, to marriage vows, to commitments to serve.

One of the most subtle New Testament paradoxes is a saying which appears only in Matthew's gospel (Mt 10:16): "Be shrewd as serpents and simple as doves." The follower of Jesus is called to blend truth-telling with prudence and with charity. In a family there are truths that are private and should not be disclosed beyond the family circle. There are hard truths too that must at times be spoken, but with humility and transparent love.

Speaking the truth is especially important in the sacrament of reconciliation or in the quest for spiritual guidance. We choose a confessor so that we might lay our sins humbly before God, confident that God's healing love comes to us through sacramental signs. We choose a "soul friend" so that, with his or her help, we might grow in the Lord's life and in discerning those things which promote the Kingdom of God. We need others to mirror back to us what is happening or not happening in our journey toward the Lord. The quality of our relationship with a confessor or spiritual guide will depend largely upon the transparency with which we disclose ourselves. It is imperative, therefore, that such a relationship be characterized by free self-disclosure and by the avoidance of "hidden corners" in our lives.

Daily events often demand a choice between honesty and evasion. Make a deliberate choice for truth. Speak and act as straightforwardly as you can, accepting responsibility for your words and actions.

At the end of the day, examine your interactions with others. From your successes and failures, learn to be transparent and truthful. Ask yourself: as a member of the Vincentian Family, does passion for the truth shine out from my life like a beacon? Let your life radiate the resolution to:

- speak the truth, especially when the truth is uncomfortable or embarrassing;

- witness to the truth, so that your life matches your words;

- search for the truth humbly as a wayfarer rather than thinking that you possess it as an "owner;"

- practice the truth through works of justice, charity, and peace;

- strive for single-minded truth, or purity of intention;

- live truthfully as a servant, having modest possessions, dressing simply, and sharing readily what you have;

- express the truth clearly, using simple, transparent language, especially when teaching others.

TRUSTING IN GOD'S PROVIDENCE

Can any of you by worrying add a moment to your lifespan? If even the smallest things are beyond your control, why are you anxious about the rest? Notice how the flowers grow. They do not toil or spin. But I tell you, not even Solomon in all his splendor was dressed like one of them. If God so clothes the grass in the field that grows today and is thrown into the oven tomorrow, will he not much more provide for you, O you of little faith? As for you, do not seek what you are to eat and what you are to drink, and do not worry anymore. All the nations of the world seek for these things, and your Father knows that you need them. Instead, seek his kingdom, and these other things will be given you besides.

Lk 12:25-31

What great hidden treasures there are in holy providence and how marvelously Our Lord is honored by those who follow it.

SV I, 68

Human experience abounds in polarities: life and death, health and sickness, grace and sin, care and neglect, plan and disruption, design and chaos, peace and violence. Trust in Providence bridges the gap between them.

Throughout his life, St. Vincent spoke of providence with great conviction. Trust in providence is inseparable from faith in a loving, personal God. It is an attitude of reverence before the mystery of God, as revealed in Christ, in whom life, death, and resurrection are integrated. Birth, death, beauty, tragedy – all these are shrouded in mystery. We continually struggle to reconcile opposites, to plumb the depths of life.

At the heart of New Testament faith is belief in a loving God, revealed as Father through his Son, Jesus, who takes on human flesh, and in dying, leaves us his Spirit. Jesus himself struggles with the mysteries of life, growth, success, betrayal, desertion by his followers, physical and psychological pain, and death. He finds the resolution of his struggle, not in some clearly stated philosophy that he outlines for future ages, but in commending himself into the hands of his Father. He trusts that his Father loves him deeply and that God can bring joy from sorrow, life from death. Jesus' death and resurrection are the ultimate proclamation of Providence.

The New Testament, reflecting on Jesus' experience, tells us again and again to focus on the personal love of God for us. The Spirit of the Father and the Son is active from the beginning, guiding the course of history. The Spirit anoints Jesus with power from on high and directs him and his disciples in their ministry. The Spirit sends Jesus to preach good news to the poor (Lk 4:18).

Jesus assures his followers of God's providence even in the worst of times: "When they lead you away and hand you over, do not worry beforehand about what you are to say. But say whatever will be given to you at that hour. For it will not be you who are speaking but the Holy Spirit." (Mk 13:11).

One of the crucial signs of faith in a personal, provident God is confident prayer. The very act of praying states that we believe that God is alive, relates to us, cares about us in our struggles, listens to us, and responds, hearing the cries of the poor especially. It is for this reason that Luke's gospel insists so frequently on trusting, persistent prayer (cf. Lk. 11:1-13; 18:1-8).

Trust in providence is the ability to hope in God's wisdom and power. It implies belief that there is an unseen wisdom that guides the events of history and that is able to reconcile opposites.

St. Paul returns frequently to the theme of the "hidden plan" of God. It is revealed in Christ, who brings together death and life, but its fullness is unveiled only in the end-time when all things are subjected to Christ and through him to the Father (1 Cor. 15:28). "[God] has made known to us the mystery of his will in accord with his favor that he set forth in [Christ] as a plan for the fullness of times, to sum up all things in him, in heaven and on earth." (Eph 1:9).

But, as the scriptures themselves state, God's wisdom remains a mystery, "a stumbling block to the Jews and foolishness to the gentiles" (1 Cor 1:23). The mystery of the cross and resurrection of Jesus, the center of our faith, provides no explanation about how life and death are reconciled. It calls us, rather, to say with Jesus: "Father, into your hands I commend my spirit" (Lk 23:46). The cross proclaims that the power of God overcomes human weakness, bringing life from death, and that the wisdom of God surpasses the limits of human reasoning, bringing light to the darkness.

Trust in providence is related to patience and perseverance. It involves patient waiting, not in immobile passivity, but in constant alertness so that we might know the right moment to act. Grace has its moments, St. Vincent tells us (SV II, 453). Sometimes the right moment comes quickly; at other times it arrives slowly. Sometimes it comes unexpectedly, with almost no preparation; at other times it reveals itself only with considerable prodding.

We are active sharers in God's providence. God acts not only upon, but in and through, us. God's freedom does not diminish, but enhances, ours. Providence, then, works not only through the events of nature and history that unfold upon us, but also through us personally. Not only is God responsible for the world, but we are too. In fact, a servant of the poor personifies God's providence in the lives of the poor.

Each person bears responsibility for himself or herself, for other individuals, for groups within society, for the political order, and for the gifts of creation. As the Church tells us, "Action on behalf of justice and participation in the transformation of the world are a constitutive element in preaching the gospel."[7]

Our own providence in looking toward the future takes nothing away from God's Providence. Rather, it manifests it. Even when we are very active, we can still thank God for the gifts that God works in and through us. "The Mighty One has done great things for me and holy is his name" (Lk 1:49).

Take time each day to be aware of God's provident love. Pay close attention to what is happening in your life. Sometimes God will come

---

[7] Synod of Bishops, 1971, *Justice in the World*, in Acta Apostolicae Sedis LXIII (1971) 924.

to you like a gentle breeze. Sometimes his intervention will be like a resounding trumpet blast. Be alert to what causes you joy and sorrow. Each day has moments in which God's providence can be discerned.

COMMUNICATING JOYFUL FAITH

Rejoice always. Pray without ceasing. In all circumstances give thanks, for this is the will of God for you in Christ Jesus.

1 Thess 5:16-18

When someone has joy in her heart, she will not be able to hide it. You will see it on her face.

SV X, 147

Those who follow Jesus see with different eyes. They believe that the coming of the Lord has ushered in a new era: the reign of God is at hand. In it the blind see, the deaf hear, the lame leap, the gentle are conquerors, sinners become saints, and the dead rise. All these gospel paradoxes, which Jesus identifies as the signs of the Kingdom, seem jarring to others.

The evangelists, especially Luke, see the world upside down, so to speak. The last will be first; the first, last. Those who save their life will lose it; those who lose their life, will save it. The humble will be exalted; the exalted, humbled. Those who mourn will rejoice; those who laugh will cry. St. Vincent believed deeply in this upside-down vision of the world.

Mary, the first disciple, exemplifies this radical faith. She believes that God casts down the mighty from their thrones and lifts up the lowly. God is utterly personal for her. The God of the Magnificat is no distant, faceless "ground of being" or "prime mover." Mary's God is not the abstract god of the philosophers. She listens to God and speaks with God. She believes that God hears her. Even more, she believes that God acts, governing human history.

She communicates her faith in this God with joy. Her Magnificat spirituality has deep roots in Old Testament passages like Psalm 136, which, in the form of a litany, recounts God's saving deeds in Israel's history, repeating after each event, "for his mercy endures forever." Mary echoes the Psalmist, who sings of God's greatness in creating the universe (136:4-9), in bringing Israel to the promised land (136:12-22), and in having pity on the misery of the chosen people (136:23-25).

Mary's faith is rooted in many other beautiful Old Testament texts which similarly chant God's praises for intervening in Israel's history, like Exodus 15:1-18, which proclaims God's greatness for delivering Israel from its captivity in Egypt, for passing through the Red Sea, for guiding the chosen people through the desert, and for bringing it to the land of Canaan.

A Magnificat spirituality is faith-filled, joyful, grateful, and deeply conscious that God loves humankind as a whole, and us individually. Mary has no doubts that the living God has entered into an intimate personal relationship with her and that God is guiding her life from its beginning to its end.

In our Vincentian Family, we strive to interpret life and events with a spirit of faith. St. Vincent urges us, as we serve the poor, to have a faith that is "living and effective" (SV II, 346). While faith is a gift, it is also a choice. It must be nourished. So we pray often, "Lord, I do believe; help my unbelief," and we commit ourselves to believing and trusting in God, even when things seem impossible.

Pray the Magnificat often. Reflect on stories from the scriptures and the lives of the saints in which God accomplishes what is unexpected. Think of times in your own life, or in the lives of people you know, where God acted in unexpected ways. Meditate on these. Believe and rejoice.

BEING GENTLE AND FIRM

Learn from me, for I am meek and humble of heart.

Mt 11:29

The Spirit of Our Lord ... is equally gentle and firm.

SV VII, 226

Learn to be gentle. Anger can be a force for good or evil in life. To channel it creatively and find appropriate ways of expressing it is a great challenge.

When directed against injustice, as Jesus' example shows, anger strengthens a person to act courageously, to confront the Pharisee, to "cast out the money-changers from the temple." But, as human experience teaches, anger can also be destructive. It can drive us to lash out at the weak or the innocent.

Learn to understand your anger and to harness it for good, for truth, for justice, and for peace. You may fail many times in your attempts, but know that the power of God is much greater than the weakness that you experience.

Jesus assures us that the gentle will be happy. Believe this word of the Lord. Gentleness wins the hearts of others. It expresses itself as approachability, warmth, openness, and deep respect for the person of others.

But the gentle person should also know how to mix the bitter with the sweet. Vincent de Paul once wrote to Louise de Marillac: "If the gentleness of your spirit needs a drop of vinegar, borrow a little of it from the spirit of Our Lord. O, Mademoiselle, how very well he knew how to find the bitter-sweet when it was necessary" (SV I, 393-94). As we carry out our mission to "build a civilization of love,"[8] finding the balance between gentleness and firmness is sometimes not easy.

Healthy Christian living involves a whole series of paradoxical qualities: simplicity and prudence, creativity and humility, initiative and docility, flexibility and stability, listening and advising, animating and directing, trusting and planning, serving and governing. Yet experience teaches us that the balance between gentleness and firmness is especially elusive. Even the most virtuous of saints struggled to find it. St. Vincent often prayed that his followers would have "the spirit of Our Lord, who was equally gentle and firm."

---

[8] Wednesday 15 December 1999, General Audience. Pope John Paul II.

The paradox gentle/firm is nowhere more evident than in the Christian call to work for justice and peace. Without justice, there is no abiding peace. But Aquinas reminds us that the passion most immediately associated with justice is anger.[9] Anger recoils in the face of injustice. It springs back in order to gather energy to strike out at what is wrong. It moves us to hunger and thirst for what is right. Such anger is born from love and respect for the human person whose rights we perceive as being violated. It strains to right wrong, to reestablish an order in which persons can grow and flourish. It will always be aroused when we perceive that unjust structures are depriving the poor of the political, social, religious, economic, or personal freedom that their human dignity demands.

The truth is that a good dose of anger is sometimes very helpful in life. Anger is creative energy. It can be used for good or for bad. The challenge is to channel it properly.

The gentle find creative ways of expressing anger in "action on behalf of justice and participation in the transformation of the world."[10] For those eager to change societal structures, education for justice and peace is a primary means for directing their anger toward good.

---

[9] Cf. Summa Theologica I-II. 46.2, 4, 6.
[10] Synod of Bishops, 1971, Justice in the World, in Acta Apostolicae Sedis, 63 (1971) 924.

In the lives of the gentle, conversation and dialogue, accompanied by suffering love, will be the principal means for settling conflicts. These are the tools that Jesus himself used; Paul tells the Ephesians that he is "our peace, who... broke down the dividing wall of enmity" (Eph 2:14). If we have a genuine passion for dialogue, justice, and peace, then our lives will be a clear sign that the Kingdom of God is at hand.

Gentleness need not, by any means, be passive. Rather, "passionate" gentleness knows how to direct anger, to channel it so that "justice rolls like a river" (Am 5:24) and becomes a mighty torrent that uproots oppressive societal structures and softens the ground so that the seeds of peace can be planted.

So, stand for justice, even if only by small acts. Say a word, write a letter, take an initiative on behalf of someone who has suffered injustice. Whether you take direct personal action or whether you express your conviction in concert with the members of our Family, transform your anger into a courageous response. Do not let pent-up anger corrode your life.

If you yourself have been wronged, choose either to be silent or to respond truthfully while trusting in God's care for you. When you point out wrongs done to you, bear in mind that you too have wronged others. Seek to forgive. Pray for those who have hurt you. "Do not let the sun set on your anger" (Eph 4:26). Let gentleness and love have the final word.

KNOWING HOW TO DIE DAILY

Then he said to all, "If anyone wishes to come after me, he must deny himself and take up his cross daily and follow me. For whoever wishes to save his life will lose it, but whoever loses his life for my sake will save it. What profit is there for one to gain the whole world yet lose or forfeit himself?"

Luke 9:23-25

Remember that we live in Jesus Christ by the death of Jesus Christ and that we are to die in Jesus Christ by the life of Jesus Christ and that our life ought to be hidden in Jesus Christ and full of Jesus Christ and that in order to die like Jesus Christ, it is necessary to live like Jesus Christ.

SV I, 295

Jesus "lays down his life for his friends" (Jn 15:13). All four evangelists build their narratives toward the climactic story of his passion and death, followed by the triumph of his resurrection.

Since apostolic times, Jesus' dying love has been the source of strength for those who have died following him. The martyr, out of love, renounces the most basic human gift: life. Some, like Polycarp, underwent a martyrdom that crowned a long life which was already strikingly holy. "I have served Christ for 86 years," Polycarp told his captors, "how could I deny my king and savior now?" For others, martyrdom was more like a "second baptism," washing away their sins, sometimes even rather notable ones, "in the blood of the lamb." Their sins paled into insignificance in the light of their martyrdom.

Every era has seen martyrs, from the proto-martyr Stephen to modern martyrs like Oscar Romero. In fact, their number has increased. The twentieth century saw more martyrs than the first.

But overall, martyrs are relatively rare. Few of us will walk that path. While we might long for the clear, simple, dramatic gesture of dying for Christ, for most of us the following of Christ will involve bearing the cross day-in and day-out over a long life with patience and fidelity. As a wise old missionary once said, "It is often harder to live for Christ than to die for him."

In fact, the root meaning of "martyrdom" is "witness" to one's faith. As the early Christians realized that relatively few would shed their blood for Christ, they began to focus more sharply on another form of dying, called asceticism or mortification. "Asceticism" means training or discipline. Christ's "athlete" seeks the laurel wreath placed on the head of the winner at the end of life's race. "I have competed well; I have finished the race; I have kept the faith. From now on the crown of righteousness awaits me" (2 Tim 4:7-8).

Ascetics adopt a simple lifestyle. They fast. Some engage in sexual abstinence. The point of such ascetical practices, in their healthiest form, is not to "give up" objects, but to reconstruct the self, to become a new person. In other words, all self-denial has growth in love as its goal. Giving things up is meaningless unless it frees one to love more deeply.

The following of Christ always involves discipline, "taking up one's cross daily" (Lk 9:23). On the list of ascetics and great lovers of the cross, one thinks spontaneously of Francis of Assisi whose life has fascinated countless Christians. He lived with wonderful simplicity, while still obviously being deeply in love with creation, praising "Brother Sun" and "Sister Moon."

Discipline helps in achieving many of the values we commit ourselves to: prayer, work, study, a simple life-style, fidelity to one's spouse and family. In fact, few values are achieved without it. In that sense, asceticism reflects grace working in our lives and helps us to mirror the constancy of God's love.

Asceticism, while not very much in vogue today, has enormous relevance in a consumer society characterized by the inequitable distribution of wealth, an entertainment culture, the desire for immediate gratification, and exploitative sexual and power relationships. The witness of a simple lifestyle, of long-lasting fidelity, and of consistent responsiveness to the needs of others, especially the poor, is a powerful sign of the presence of the Kingdom of God.

Simplicity of life opens us up to a deeper appreciation of God's gifts. A simple meal, eaten slowly in conversation with others, can become a feast of flavor, companionship, and the awareness of God's goodness.

Among the ascetical practices that can be helpful in today's world are those that follow:

- Work hard as servants do.

- Be faithful to the duties of your state in life – whether married or single – and give them preference when they conflict with other more enticing matters. Reach out to others in your family, at work, and elsewhere, even when you find it inconvenient.

- Use time well. It is a gift. Avoid squandering it. Schedule your time. Be sure to budget sufficient time for prayer, work, companionship, and relaxation.

- Praise God faithfully in the morning and in the evening. Pray in a disciplined way, set time aside for it daily, and encourage family members to do so too.

- Be modest in regard to material possessions, like clothing, or cars, or other items. Care for them well. Develop a simple life-style. This form of asceticism is very difficult in contemporary society, which urges you again and again to have more.

- When making decisions about acquiring personal possessions, consider not just what you want, but what you need. Choose things that fulfill your family's needs and that enable you to work efficiently and well. Be grateful for what you have. Curb the desire always to have more. Be a wise steward of God's gifts, sharing them graciously with others. In doing so, give not just your gift but yourself. Use material things to foster your relationships, especially with your family, friends, and the poor around you. Thank God who provides for your daily needs.

- Be disciplined in eating and drinking, and avoid anxiety or complaining about what you eat or what you drink. The key is moderation. A healthy asceticism in regard to eating and drinking can be an aid in keeping one's weight down and staying in good physical condition.

- Be disciplined in the use of alcohol. Immoderate drinking often causes ill health, unreliability at work, and family strife. Many who have experienced difficulties in regard to marital fidelity testify that sexual problems began or evolved when their inhibitions had been lowered by drinking too much. As in so many things, moderation is the key when it comes to drinking.

- Develop a critical sense in using television, radio, movies, computers, the phone, and other media. What we take in through the senses, especially if it is a steady diet, inevitably influences our conduct bit by bit. Recognize both the positive and negative influence that the various media can have. Enjoy the benefits of the media. Avoid those that promote gratuitous sex or violence and that otherwise degrade human dignity. Budget the time you spend in using them. Be moderate in their use.

- Withhold negative criticism and divisive words. St. Benedict said that murmuring was the greatest vice in monasteries. It is also destructive in families and in work-situations. A healthy norm is to withhold critical words unless you can speak them constructively to someone who can do something to correct the situation.

- Develop a balanced life-style. Recognize your own limitedness as a creature and know that God works not only through you, but also without you. When we are worn out, difficulties that at other times might more easily be handled become insurmountable problems. Listen to your body, know when tiredness is sapping your strength, and be alert to the signs that signal exhaustion, like irritability, anger or poor judgment.

- Observe Sunday as the Lord's Day. Choose to make it, first of all, a day of praise and thanksgiving to God in the Eucharist. Celebrate it as a member of the Body of Christ; lift up your heart to the Lord in communion with others. Learn how to rest. In Old Testament times, even slaves were free on the Lord's Day. Try not to conduct business on Sunday. Make it a day of relaxation and togetherness with family and friends, or with those who have neither. Prepare a special family meal. Listen to joyful music. Engage in recreational activity. Whatever you do, whether alone or with others, do it in a spirit of joy and deep gratitude to God.

Often the most important ascetical practices are not those we choose on our own initiative but those that life thrusts upon us, like keeping vigil with a sick child or a dying friend, or fasting while we are eating on the run as we try to serve the poor. St. Vincent tells us: "Patience is the virtue of the perfect. What consolation one has when she has suffered something for the love of God!" (SV X, 181).

As is the case with so many good things, there is a danger in asceticism too. Ascetics run the risk of Pelagianism, a fifth-century error that St. Augustine combated strenuously but that continually re-emerges. It proposes an athletic view of salvation, the tendency to think that if you "train" well enough, you will win the race. Ascetics can become proud of their "works." They can become hard on others who seem less disciplined. But ultimately, holiness is a gift from God, not an ascetical achievement. Only the humble are able to receive it.

PERSEVERING TO THE END

They will look upon his face, and his name will be on their foreheads. Night will be no more, nor will they need light from lamp or sun, for the Lord God shall give them light, and they shall reign forever and ever.

Rev 22:4-5

We have reason to praise God for this: by God's goodness and mercy there are among us sick and dying members who transform their pain and suffering into a theater of patience, in which all their virtues shine out radiantly.

SV XI, 73

The cross and resurrection stand at the center of the good news. For the New Testament writers, Jesus must not escape his hour. He must undergo the cross if he is to enter into his glory. His followers too must take up their cross daily. But the cross of Christ, as well as that of his followers, is always viewed from the perspective of resurrection faith.

Using a hymn, Paul calls us to identify with the "self-emptying" Christ, who has become one of us. *"Have among yourselves the same attitude that is also yours in Christ Jesus, Who, though he was in the form of God, did not regard equality with God something to be grasped. Rather, he emptied himself, taking the form of a slave, coming in human likeness; and found human in appearance, he humbled himself, becoming obedient to death, even death on a cross. Because of this, God greatly exalted him and bestowed on him the name that is above every name, that at the name of Jesus every knee should bend, of those in heaven and on earth and under the earth, and every tongue confess that Jesus Christ is Lord!" (Phil 2:5-11)*

The Christian journey focuses on conformity with the self-giving Lord: "I have been crucified with Christ; yet I live, no longer I, but Christ lives in me; insofar as I now live in the flesh, I live by faith in the Son of God who has loved me and given himself up for me" (Gal 2:19-20). Paul clearly affirms that the person who lives and dies with Christ has a new source of inner energy: the glorified Lord, who has become a life-giving Spirit (1 Cor 15:45).

For the author of Hebrews, the prospective joy of the resurrection gives new meaning to the cross. He presents Jesus, who now sits at the right hand of the Father, as the model for endurance in the face of hardship and encourages us by Jesus' example to persevere until the triumphant end of the race: "Let us keep our eyes fixed on Jesus, who is the leader and perfecter of faith. For the sake of the joy that lay before him he endured the cross, despising its shame" (Heb 12:2).

St. Vincent, who placed great emphasis on the cross, maintained a strong resurrection faith throughout his life. Since he lived 30 years beyond the median age of death at that time, he saw most of his closest friends die before him. Shortly before he died, he told his followers that, for the last eighteen years, he had never gone to bed at night without preparing for death. As the end approached, he said to a small group gathered around him: "To be consumed for God, to have no goods nor power except for the purpose of consuming them for God. That is what our Savior did himself, who was consumed for love of his Father" (SV XIII, 179).

As a help in persevering to the end:

• Meditate often on the passion narratives, particularly on Fridays.

• Reflect on where the cross appears in your daily life. What illness, what troubling situation, person or event is your cross today? What events humble you? What injustice do you or the members of your family suffer? Is death near to you or to others close to you? How well prepared are you to stand before the Lord?

- Meditate on the resurrection. Let resurrection faith give you strength in adversity. Think of times, in your experience, when life has overcome death, when good has overcome evil, and when hope has overcome despair. Let Easter faith predominate and "Alleluia" be your grateful song.

AFTERWORD

*May the God of peace himself make you
perfectly holy and may you entirely, spirit,
soul, and body, be preserved blameless for
the coming of our Lord Jesus Christ. The
one who calls you is faithful, and he will
also accomplish it.*

1 Thess 5: 23-24

*O, how little it takes to be very holy – to do
the will of God in all things.*

SV II, 36

Jesus proclaims a universal call to holiness, a universal call to mission, and a universal call to build a civilization of love.

It is not just religious or priests whom the Lord asks to be faith-filled followers. While they have a special role to play in the Church, all lay women and men do too.

This Rule aims to assist the many lay members of our Vincentian Family as they seek to follow Christ, the Evangelizer and Servant of the Poor, faithfully. It describes a way of holiness that countless generous men and women in our Family have already walked, and still do. Such "saints" teach us much more by their witness than by their words, much more by their life than by their lessons, much more by their person than by their projects.

In our Family, genuinely holy people will consistently connect the soul of the Church with the soul of the world. They will blend deep rootedness in God with deep rootedness in the sufferings of the poor. They will express a creative, contemporary sense of tradition in complex, changing circumstances.

As we journey together in the Church and in our Vincentian Family, the life of the Spirit is essential. Holiness is not just being an extraordinary worker. Nor is it just being pious. It is being "possessed by God." Holy men or women radiate God's presence. People sense God in them. They communicate God's joy, God's strength, God's peace, and God's daily care within their own homes, and they carry those same gifts into the lives of those around them, especially the poor. The challenge for each of us in our Vincentian Family is to be spirit-filled ourselves and, together, to create spirit-filled communities and associations:

- where evangelical charity reigns among us and then radiates out to others around us

- where we speak the truth among ourselves with simplicity, humility, and constancy, and then speak it with those outside in the same way

- where we pray faithfully with each other, and then share our prayer naturally with others too

- where we support one another and enjoy one another's company as genuine friends, and then share that friendship with our acquaintances and with the poor who surround us

- where we listen well to each other and discern the will of God together, and then are also able to listen well to the deepest cries of humanity and discern the will of God with the "the least of our brethren"

- where we renounce immediate gratification for the sake of life's more important goals, and then manifest to those around us, by our lives, what life's most important goals really are.

At the end of this Rule, let me say a final word of encouragement to all the lay members of our Family as you strive to walk in the way of the Lord. Follow the Lord with confidence, courage and joy. Let him be the Rule in your life. And let your light shine out in the world, so that others, seeing how you live the gospels, will believe deeply and will also, like you, make their belief concrete through practical works of justice, love and peace.